AF382226

GETTING READY FOR YOUR BABY

How to welcome the new addition to your family

Written by Dominque van der Kaa
In collaboration with Carole Bloch
Translated by Ciaran Traynor

Health and Wellbeing 50MINUTES.com

50MINUTES.com
HEALTH AND WELLBEING
WITHOUT THE HEADACHE
STOP PROCRASTINATING - RIGHT NOW!
Beat your procrastination habit once and for all
NOW
Health and Wellbeing
50MINUTES.com
Make learning fun!
Learn to love yourself
Dealing with bullying at school
Your guide to making friends
www.50minutes.com

FURTHER READING 73

GETTING READY FOR YOUR BABY

- **Problem**: you are finally pregnant, and you are very excited about your baby. Nevertheless, you are plagued by worries and feel overwhelmed with questions: how can I get ready for the arrival of this baby? What do I have to do before they come to make them feel at home? How am I going to get organised when they will be there?
- **Aims**: although this guide is mainly for expectant mothers, it aims to help both parents to prepare, materially and psychologically, for the arrival of their new baby in order to welcome it as best they can.
- **FAQs**:
  - When should I tell my boss I'm pregnant?
  - How should I choose my paediatrician?
  - When should I register my baby in a crèche?
  - How can I get over the baby blues?
  - How should I prepare myself if I have twins?
  - What will happen if my baby is premature?

- What are the obligatory vaccinations for babies?
- How can I prepare my older children for the arrival of their new brother or sister?
- How can I get my dog ready for the arrival of the baby?

Welcoming your baby means giving them a pregnancy that is full of love and kindness. It also means anticipating their future needs in order to get ready for this extraordinary adventure that you and your family are about to experience. The parents-to-be will therefore find in this guide a whole range of advice to help them to get their house ready, plan what will be necessary for the newborn and deal with the pregnancy period as best they can, in order to be psychologically prepared to give their baby the time and attention it needs. This guide will also attempt to provide some answers to the questions which often arise over the weeks before and after the birth.

DEALING WITH YOUR PREGNANCY AND PREPARING TO GIVE BIRTH

WELLBEING ABOVE ALL

Although being pregnant is not an illness, women are advised to see a gynaecologist as soon as possible. Your baby's happiness starts with your wellbeing. Take care of yourself: eat a balanced diet, go easy on fatty, sugary foods and fizzy drinks so as not to gain more weight than you have to, and drink a litre and a half of water a day. Try to avoid overly strenuous sports, and do some walking, swimming, water aerobics or prenatal aerobics instead. Take it easy as often as you can at work, when you move around and when you go out.

The future father also has a role to play in this adventure. He will be anxious too. Ask him if he wants to come with you to your prenatal consultations or childbirth classes. Of course, you will no doubt both be involved in getting the baby's room ready, but do not stop there: read books together about pregnancy, giving birth and your first interactions with your baby.

sudden cravings, backaches, disturbed sleep, mood swings, weight gain, and so on. Their symptoms disappear after the birth of the baby, at the very latest. This syndrome shows the father's desire to take part in the pregnancy as much as he can and is a way of externalising his fears about becoming a parent.

Some maternity wards offer preparation classes for the arrival of your baby. These classes give expectant parents information on pregnancy and how the birth process and post-natal period will go. They therefore allow the future mother – and possibly the future father as well – to be less anxious about the unknown experience of giving birth. You will learn muscle and breathing exercises that you can practice at home and that will help you throughout your pregnancy and labour. These classes are collective and friendly. Future parents will be given answers to their questions and meet other couples who are also expecting a baby, and can therefore bond and grow closer with them. You will also become more confident about the thought of becoming a parent.

You can also try other methods depending on your temperament or your preferences, such as sophrology, yoga, aquatic preparation, prenatal singing and haptonomy. These methods offer different tools to become aware of your body and its tensions. They will give you a sense of wellbeing and relax your muscles, as well as giving you a special moment of contact with the unborn baby.

Moreover, in order to feel mentally and physically healthy, there are some gentle gymnastic exercises and simple breathing techniques that you can do at home. Before doing them, speak to your gynaecologist during one of your appointments to make sure that they do not advise against it. Never overdo it during these exercises and do not obstruct your breathing.

A few gentle exercises	
Breathing exercises	**Gymnastic exercises**
• Breathe deeply for around ten minutes. The deeper you breathe, the more muscles you will use. • Breathe, inflating your stomach, then breathe out slowly while gently bringing your stomach back in. • Get down on all fours with your legs slightly spread, your arms tense, your hands and your back straight. Breathe in and curve your back while breathing out. Repeat this exercise five to ten times.	• Stretch yourself out on your back on the floor, with your arms along your body, your knees bent and the soles of your feet pressed against the floor. Lift both feet, then lower them again. Repeat five times. • Sit crossed-legged with your back straight, push your legs slightly downwards with your hands and breathe out. Repeat five times.

GETTING READY FOR YOUR STAY IN HOSPITAL

You should also waste no time in choosing your maternity ward. A good maternity ward should offer not only a capable obstetric team, but also give you a warm, personalised welcome as well as a high degree of comfort. Word of mouth can help you to make this decision, but if you already have an obstetrician or gynaecologist, it would be natural for them to take care of you throughout your pregnancy. They will most likely suggest the maternity ward where they work or a maternity ward with a neonatology branch, in case there is a problem when you give birth.

Do not forget that, in some maternity wards, you will have to register early. During this registration, do not hesitate to ask to visit the ward and learn about how it works (labour techniques, whether or not there is a paediatrician, and so on).

Do not wait for the first contractions to prepare your hospital suitcase. The ideal is to pack it a month before the due date. Most maternity wards supply a list of useful things for the mother and her new baby. If yours does not, make a little checklist with your partner to be sure that you will not forget anything. Moreover, organise yourself so that you will have less to do during your first few weeks after getting back from the hospital: ask your family and friends for help, stock your freezer before leaving, have a supply of bathroom products and nappies, and so on.

PREPARING YOUR BABY'S WORLD

When you are thinking about how to welcome your newborn home, try to create a warm environment where they will feel comfortable, which may encourage them to be more independent and mean that they will wake up feeling safe. This environment has to make them want to discover and take an interest in everything going on around them.

Ideally, you should get everything ready well before you give birth. This will allow you not only to be available and be able to give all your attention to your new baby, but also to air the room and the new furniture for some time (at least a month) before the arrival of your baby and limit the damage of possible pollutants used to make them.

You will have the choice between new furniture or second-hand items, but whichever one you choose, the equipment must be made with your baby's comfort in mind and be suitable for their age and development. Be particularly vigilant regarding their health (watch out for toxic paint!) and safety. You should therefore go for toys made to European, or even British, standards. Learn how to use every new piece of equipment before setting it up for your child and regularly check its condition. Of course, do not forget that you should also buy things which you like and which are suited to your needs (ease of use, budget, space available in the room, and so on). A good thing to remember is that you can buy convertible furniture, which will prevent you from spending all your money buying things for your baby as they get bigger.

| Evolving bed.

THE BEDROOM

The layout of the room

A baby's room will quickly become their little kingdom. They will spend a lot of time there, and it is therefore essential that it has everything they need from their very first day at home.

Choose a quiet room, beside the garden if possible, so your child can listen to the calls of birds, the rustling of leaves in the wind, and so on. The temperature of the room should ideally be between 18 and 20°C. Create a calm, relaxing environment, preferably with pastel-coloured walls. Opt for an off-white ceiling, which will give a warmer hint to the room. You should not go overboard with wall decorations either: choose a few attractive objects that are suitable for your child's size and development. If possible, avoid carpets, which are a haven for mites, and tiles, which are cold to walk on and do not offer a very soft landing in the case of a fall. A better choice would be linoleum or laminate, which is easy to maintain.

You should also think about quickly getting rid of any potential dangers by putting covers on electronic sockets, protecting the corners of furniture with special padding, making doors safer with door stops, and so on. Another useful precaution is to avoid putting furniture under the windows in order to avoid accidents in the case of climbing.

If possible, organise the room into four different spaces: a sleeping space, a feeding section, a place to play and a corner to change, wash and dress your baby. Of course, you could also have a space in your bathroom to wash your baby, and you could feed them in your bedroom or in the living room. The playing area could also be elsewhere.

The essentials

The bed should be out of draughts. To help you to find a good location, try to sleep in the place where you are thinking about putting your baby. This will give you a better idea of the light that will fall on your baby's face and allow you to see what they will see when they wake up.

SOME EXTRA ADVICE

In the first few days, you can put the carry-cot or Moses basket on the mattress of your baby's cot. In this way, your newborn will feel safely wrapped up, and you will be able to move them about easily without waking them up if need be. You can use Moses baskets up until your baby is around three months old.

Cribs and bedside cribs (a crib open on one side, which – as its name suggests – allows you to attach your baby's bed to your own) can be used up until the age of six months, or when your baby is able to sit up by themselves. If you buy a bedside crib, make sure that its mattress is at the same height as your own. The bars of the crib should not be any more than 6 cm apart.

| Bedside crib.

A cot can be used until your baby is ready to sleep in a real bed. Cot bars should be between 2.5 cm and 6.5 cm apart. There are also cots with adjustable mattress heights, and you can even buy foldable, transportable beds for the occasional trip.

For each bed or cradle model, make sure that the bedding is correctly attached by placing the straps on the outside of the bed in order to avoid danger. You should also check the size of the mattress, because it should be suitable for the size of the bed. The mattress should be firm in order to avoid the risk of suffocation. You should cover it with a thick cotton mattress protector underneath a light-coloured sheet, as they are better for relaxing and sleep than brightly co-loured sheets. You can also put a smaller cotton sheet (60x80 cm) on top, which will be easier to change. Make sure you buy enough of all of these sheets so you will be able to change them regularly without having to spend all of your time doing the washing.

In order to minimise the risk of sudden infant death syndrome, it is advised to avoid a pillow or a quilt until the age of 18 months, because babies can suffer from hyperthermia (since they still cannot regulate their body temperature) and may suffocate if they slip under it without being able to get back out again. Try using a baby sleep bag instead (a sort of bag made of quilted mate-rial, which is washable and leaves the shoulders uncovered) or a fleece over-pyjama suit (which is worn over your baby's pyjamas). If you use a blanket, never tuck it in.

| Over-pyjamas.

To add the finishing touch to the sleeping corner, buy a bedside lamp and hang a mobile above the bed, about 30 cm away from your baby's eyes, because their visual field is very limited when they are born.

You will also need a baby monitor. The model will depend on what suits you: there are ones that are bigger or smaller and easier or harder to transport; some have to be plugged in, while others work with ordinary or rechargeable batteries; some are just audio-based while others also have video; the indicators can be sounds and/or lights; and so on. The best place for a baby monitor is a metre away from the bed or even further, and make sure to buy a low-frequency or low-power model in order to limit your baby's exposure to electromagnetic waves. Do not rely on the device entirely, because it could break or be badly designed, so you should always be vigilant. Of course, try to turn it off when you are not using it.

When your baby arrives

- Always lie them down on their back. Why? Because this position makes it easier for them to breathe and regulate their temperature, and prevents some cases of asphyxiation (airways blocked by the mattress or the edge of the bed, for example).
- Do not put plush animals, toys or objects with cords – such as bibs, teething toys or

music boxes – in your baby's bed.
- Air the room on a daily basis, even in winter: you just need one to three minutes to improve the air quality if you manage to get a good current of air.
- Vacuum the mattress regularly in order to reduce the presence of mites.
- As a precaution, try to expose your baby to electronic waves (such as GSM, Wi-Fi and baby monitors) as little as possible, because specialists are still unsure how harmful they are for infants.

Your baby will take a while to realise the different between day and night. In order to help them to do so, try to dim the room when you put them to sleep during the day and have them sleep in the dark at night.

THE TOILET

Changing your baby's clothes and bathing them

There are changing tables combined with a little bath than you can put on your own bathtub, attach to the wall, and so on. Buy one that is at a comfortable height for you, preferably with rims for extra security, and follow the manufacturer's instructions. Do not forget to jam the wheels if your table has one when you use it. You can also put a baby-changing mat covered with a terry towel on a stable table or a piece of furniture.

The changing table should allow you to have everything you need within arm's reach without having to leave your child. You should also buy a little pedal bin with the right sized bin liners and stock up on nappies. Keep them under the table if possible, with a dirty linen basket for the used nappies nearby. Place a container with several toiletry products beside the table or above it, on a shelf.

Bathroom checklist	
	Bath thermometer
	Body thermometer
	Little natural sponge or washing mitt
	Gentle baby soap and shampoo
	Hair bristle-brush
	Calming, hydrating cream for irritated bottoms
	Sweet almond oil
	Cotton wool
	Physiological saline to wash your baby's eyes and nose (you can buy little one-time-use capsules)
	Nail clippers
	Special moisturising baby milk (an optional extra)

For your baby's bath, try to buy a model made out of polypropylene or recycled materials to minimise pollutants. Base your choice on the amount of room you have at home (bath on top of an adult bath, changing table with built-in bath, and so on). Always follow the safety recommendations. Inflatable or folding baths should only be used occasionally (when travelling, for example), because they are unstable, difficult to empty and difficult to dry, and therefore quickly become mouldy. You can also wash your baby in a regular bath, although this will make things more awkward for you. If you choose to do so, put a non-slip mat inside the bath to stop your baby from sliding around.

WHEN YOUR BABY ARRIVES

- Always check the temperature of the water before bathing your newborn, either with a bath thermometer or with your elbow.
- Never leave your baby unattended.
- Wash all the bath equipment well to prevent the development of mould (toys, non-slip mat, bathtub, drains).

The wardrobe

Keep your baby's nappies and a small selection of clothes in a wardrobe or chest of drawers with drawers that open easily. For greater peace of mind, try closing the bottom drawer so your child will not get stuck underneath when they begin to climb. Choose comfortable clothes which are easy to put on and are made out of soft, natural material. Be aware that you will have to change your baby several times a day, because they can spit milk on themselves, get their clothes wet or dirty, and so on. That said, do not forget that buying too much newborn clothing is pointless, because babies grow and get heavier very quickly.

Newborn clothing checklist	
	Six to eight cotton vests which fasten at the back or stomach with matching underpants, or six to eight cotton footies which open between the legs (which is very practical to stop your baby's stomach from being exposed)
	Four or five pairs of trousers
	Six to eight T-shirts (short- or long-sleeved depending on when they are born) or vests (made from wool or another natural material, depending on the season)
	Six to eight sets of pyjamas or full-body sleep suits made out of soft velvet
	A few pairs of socks and slippers – newborns' feet get cold quickly
	One or two cardigans, with the thickness depending on the season
	One hat and one outfit for their first trip out of the house, which should be lightweight and easy to dress your baby in.

MEALTIMES

Choose an armchair you feel comfortable in to breastfeed or bottle-feed your baby, with a little table by your side with a box of tissues on it. You can also settle yourself into a hammock chair hanging from the ceiling, which will both rock you and calm your baby, because it will remind them of being inside the womb.

DID YOU KNOW?

When you breastfeed or bottle-feed your baby, it is essential to move them from one arm to another in order to develop their auditory system on both sides.

Even if you plan on breastfeeding your baby, prepare two or three bottles just in case: you can use them to give your baby water. If you are not breastfeeding, you will need closer to eight bottles.

There are lots of different models, but the ideal bottle will be the one that your baby prefers! Glass bottles are better for infants because they limit their exposure to the chemical substances which can sometimes be found in plastic bottles. However, plastic bottles are lighter, unbreakable and easier for children to hold when they get bigger.

Dummies can be made out of silicon or rubber. However, once they start to be used, silicon dummies will harden and rubber dummies will grow sticky, so you should try to replace them frequently. Moreover, make sure you replace your baby's bottle as soon as it shows signs of wear.

On another note, breast pumps are sometimes necessary to relieve breast tension and extract milk, in case the newborn has to go to hospital, for example. There are manual models for occasional use and electric ones for more frequent use. These can often be rented from the maternity ward, a pharmacy or cooperatives. In order to use the breast pump correctly, ask a nurse or another breast-feeding specialist to show you how.

Finally, make sure you have at least a dozen bibs as well as a bottle warmer (unless you decide to use the microwave). Do not forget to check the temperature of the milk each time before you give it to your child. A steriliser is not necessary as long as you clean the bottle well after each use with special bottle brushes. However, if you want to play it safe, use a steriliser and always follow the instruction manual. Cold water sterilisation is also very easy to do with tablets which dissolve in cold water. You can buy these at a pharmacy.

THE SPACE TO PLAY AND EXPLORE

Prepare a spot where your child will want to spend time alone discovering their surroundings, which will allow them to explore while remaining safe. The space has to be adapted to your child's development and must obviously allow you to keep an eye on them. Leave three or four toys at most in this area, because there is no point in overwhelming them. Choose a rug to put on the floor to mark out their space, in front of a mirror which will give them an overall view of the room and allow them to see themselves. You should also have a low shelf or a basket on the ground where you can tidy away their toys, at a height that they will be able to reach when they are older so they can begin playing by themselves.

Playpens give newborns a secure playing space away from the dangers of pets and the cold of the ground. Certain playpens have an adjustable bottom that you can change as your baby develops. In any case, make sure you choose a pen with bars spaced between 4.5 and 6.5 cm apart.

Baby bouncers should only be used for short periods of time, because the newborn cannot move about freely. You should always attach your baby, ideally in a harness with a buckle between their legs so they do not slip out. Never put your baby bouncer in a high spot (such as on a table) because, if your baby makes any sudden moves, it may fall, taking your newborn with it.

Special baby poufs are very comfortable for little ones, but should only be used for short durations (around ten minutes), because they restrict movement.

GOOD TO KNOW

Babies need to be left on the floor, on their back or on their stomach as much as possible in order to be able to move about freely, as this is essential to their development. Spending too much time in a baby bouncer, a pouf or even a baby walker will prevent them from doing this. Moreover, car seats should also only be used in the car, because they stop children from moving their heads and can lead to flat head syndrome.

Similarly, avoid leaving your baby for too long in a playpen, because they will be unable to explore the space as they want to.

As for games, opt for toys with a black and white contrast rather than different colours for the first month, because babies cannot distinguish between colours until they are older. Mobiles are among the very first games that can be given to a baby. The most suitable model for infants, usable from the age of around three weeks, is the Munari mobile, a mobile with a glass ball and black and white geometric shapes, which is so simple that you can even make it yourself. At around six weeks old, you can give your child a mobile with the three primary colours.

You should also try to find baby toys which make sounds and music, in order to awaken your child's senses.

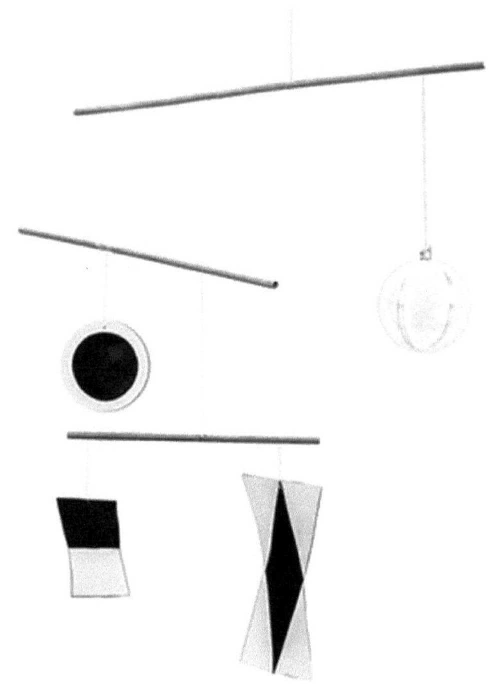

| The Munari mobile.

GOING FOR A WALK

If you want to take your baby out for some fresh air, you will have to buy yourself a buggy. There is a huge variety of different models – if your budget allows it, make sure that yours has all the functions that you may need: storage capacity, ability to fit in your car boot, easy use in public transport, during walks in the countryside and on narrow pavements, and so on. Check that it is easy to steer, that it is comfortable for your child, whether or not the back reclines, to what extent the frame can be folded up, and so on. You should also think about buying the appropriate accessories depending on the weather: an umbrella when it is hot, a cover for the rain, a mosquito net in the summer and a buggy bag (a quilted bag which you can put your baby into) for when it is cold.

Baby carriers and baby slings can also be used for walks, particularly since experts are beginning to recommend them more and more often because of the benefits they can have for the baby. In any case, you should respect each model's weight limit and make sure your baby stays in the right position. The ideal way to learn how to use them is to go to information sessions.

You will also need to think about a way to transport your baby by car. The law requires that children travel in a car seat. No matter the type of car seat, or car bed, all models must comply with European standards. Above all, the type of seat must be adapted to the size and weight of the child. This is why car seats are classified into different groups (for example, the 0+ group is suitable for a baby from birth to 13 kg) and this must be respected. The seat must be correctly installed in the car, and the child should be securely fastened according to the instruction manual.

There are two types of systems: Isofix and I-Size, which are not obligatory but which, in relation to seats which are only attached with a belt, offer an extra layer of security: the IsoFix systems allows you to fix the car seat directly into the car, while the i-Size system allows you to put your baby in the front of the car with their back to their road. They can be used until the age of 15 months and offer a maximum degree of protection.

Weigh up the seat before you buy it, because you will have to transport it regularly and the combined weight of the infant and the seat can sometimes become very heavy!

The safest position for your baby is the middle seat in the back of the car, because the infant will be at less risk if there is an accident, particularly in the case of a side collision. However, the back seat must have an appropriate seatbelt. Moreover, it is also the place that is most difficult to access, which can discourage you when it comes to fastening your child in.

You can also legally put your child in the front of the car if you fasten them in well and deactivate the passenger airbag.

Make sure you always have the belt buckles flat and tight around your baby's body. You should be able to just fit your finger underneath the belt and no more. The same goes for a baby bed, where your child should be well attached in their basket.

THE NEW ARRIVAL

THE BIRTH

If your contractions have been coming at regular intervals for at least an hour and your waters have broken, then it is time to head to the hospital.

When you reach the maternity ward, you will be examined by the obstetrician or a midwife. You will be monitored and, depending on the results, they will decide whether or not to keep you in. If you go into labour, you will be put into a room and asked if you would like an epidural anaesthetic. As a general rule, a person (the partner or a close friend or relative) is allowed to stay with the future mother until she gives birth.

SOME EXTRA ADVICE

Many future fathers are better off not being there during the birth, because they will see it as a violent and traumatising ordeal where they feel useless, powerless and unable to relieve their partner's pain. Being

When the cervix is completely dilated, the big moment arrives. You will then be taken into the delivery room and asked to push at each contraction. And, finally, out comes your baby! The umbilical cord will be cut and the new baby will often be put on your stomach for its first skin-to-skin contact, which is a very important moment which will allow them to feel certain sensations that they experienced when they were in your womb (the beating of your heart, your body heat, rocking, and so on) and therefore come into the world feeling calm and reassured. Next, the placenta separates from the wall of the uterus and is expulsed: this is the final stage of labour.

After the birth, the midwife will take your baby for its first medical exam (in order to evaluate its tone, breathing, cardiac rhythm, skin colour and reflexes). Afterwards, the mother is normally asked if she wants to breastfeed her baby for the first time.

THE IMPORTANCE OF THE AFTER-BIRTH PERIOD

During the first few days, weeks and months after the birth, you will create what is called an "attachment style" with your newborn baby, depending on the way that you talk to them, look at them and respond to their signals.

These verbal and non-verbal exchanges with the mother and father encourage the so-called "safe" development (which is to say that these exchanges develop a strong sense of security) of your baby. You should therefore be very attentive to them, because babies are extremely sensitive to other people's emotions and understand what you are saying to them from a very young age.

You will probably stay in the maternity ward for three or four days, or sometimes longer, such as in the case of a caesarean. Both you and your baby will be examined daily by a paediatrician. This stay at the hospital will allow you to get to know your child better; you can ask for advice on how to care for them, feed them, and so on. Try to rest up before going home, and try to avoid too many visits.

WELCOME HOME!

And there you are back home. A little worn out and your heads full of questions, you and your partner are probably wondering how exactly you are going to handle this crying baby who you have been left with without an instruction manual in sight. Do not worry, there is no such thing as a perfect parent and, little by little, you will begin to feel more at ease in your role as mother and father. You will get to know your baby and learn to interpret their desires, their wants and their character.

THE KEY WORDS: ORGANISATION AND REST!

- Share out household tasks with your partner and do not hesitate to ask your friends and family for help with gro-

cery shopping, chores, the washing up, cooking, and so on. Your parents will probably be more than happy to support you!
- Try to adopt your baby's rhythm by taking a nap when they go to sleep.
- Simplify your life by doing as little housework as possible.
- Limit visits if they exhaust you.

The arrival of a new child modifies a couple's dynamic. The baby occupies a central place in the family and demands a lot of attention and care in the first few weeks. Afterwards, intimacy between partners becomes rarer. Even if the future father is fully invested during the pregnancy, getting the bedroom ready, going to the ultrasounds and childbirth classes and even feeling the unborn baby move around in his partner's stomach, he will only truly meet his child after they are born, while his partner will have already lived with them for nine months. He will also have apprehensions and be asking himself questions. Paternity leave will allow him to get to know his child and support his partner. To help everything go well, the couple have to be able to talk about their expectations and what they can do to get involved, and be able to support one another. It is also essential to find time just for the two of you, where you can relax, go out, and so on.

GOING BACK TO WORK

You should think about childcare very early on in your pregnancy. Discuss it with those around you: other people might be able to advise you. Choose a place near your home, with hours that suit your own. Meet the people who will be looking after your baby and read the welcome pamphlet and the rules. Make sure that the crèche or nursery has a license. Go for a place where you are welcomed warmly and given a complete tour. Put your child down on the waiting list in the fourth month of your pregnancy.

When you return to work, a short adaptation period will be necessary (possibly for you more than your baby). Do not get yourself worked up. Do not forget that your baby can sense your emotions. Going back to work is a normal part of the birth process and should be treated as such.

Trust the person who will be looking after your

child. Let your baby try something new. Talk to them and tell them that you are sad that you have to leave them for a few hours. Make sure you say goodbye to them. At night, when you go to pick them up, tell them how happy you are to see them again and give them time to get used to things at home again. Let them take their cuddly toy with them as a link between home and the crèche or nursery. If saying goodbye to each other is difficult, giving them something that you have worn (such as a scarf) will reassure them.

GOOD TO KNOW

As previously mentioned, babies understand what you are telling them as soon as they are born. Speaking to them is extremely important: do not hesitate to explain to them what you are in the middle of doing (bathing them, feeding them, changing them, making their dinner, taking them to nursery, who will come to get them at night, and so on). These exchanges will reassure them and will therefore allow them to feel safe even though you are being separated.

FAQS

WHEN SHOULD I TELL MY BOSS I'M PREGNANT?

If you are employed you should let your boss know as soon as you find out you are pregnant, because this will trigger different legal protections to look after your health and the health of your unborn child, while also ensuring that you will have good working conditions.

To inform your employer, you can give them a medical certificate (indicating your pregnancy and due date) by registered letter, or hand it to them yourself, making sure to ask for acknowledgement of receipt.

You will then be given:

- Paid time off for antenatal care.
- Paid maternity leave.
- Protection against unfair treatment, discrimination or dismissal.
- A risk assessment by your employer, in order

to identify any health and safety risks to you and your baby, including long hours or heavy lifting. If there are any risks, your employer should change your working conditions: for example, they may alter your working hours or allow you to work at home from time to time. If they cannot do so, then they are obliged to offer you a different job for the duration of your pregnancy. If there is no other job you can do, you have the right to stay at home until they have found a solution.

You may also be entitled to extra rights beyond the legal minimum, depending on your contract.

HOW SHOULD I CHOOSE MY PAEDIATRICIAN?

A paediatrician is a doctor who specialises in child and infant care. In some maternity wards, they are even present during childbirth. You should therefore think about this during your pregnancy. To choose one, ask yourself the following questions:

- Do you want them to be attached to a hospital in your region?

- Would you prefer a man or a woman?
- Does their age matter to you?
- Do you want a paediatrician who practices alternative medicine such as homeopathy?

Ask people you know for recommendations – word of mouth is often the best way to find a paediatrician. Speak to your GP, as they might also have some helpful advice. Your GP could even look after your baby. Besides medical knowledge, there are a few criteria to take into consideration.

- Choose a paediatrician not too far from where you live to avoid long journeys with your baby – you will have to make the trip at least once a month during the first year.
- Check the paediatrician's availability:
  - how long it takes to arrange a meeting,
  - the waiting time before the consultation,
  - if they can see your child in an emergency.
- The paediatrician's personality is also very important, both in their relationship with the parents and how they interact with the newborn. You have to be able to trust them, because they should not only be attentive to your baby's health and development, but

should also be there to listen to your own worries.

WHEN SHOULD I REGISTER MY BABY IN A CRÈCHE?

It is best to start thinking about a crèche as soon as possible, from the third or four month of your pregnancy, because demand is often far greater than the available space.

Bear in mind that putting your name on the waiting list is not the same as getting in. Do not hesitate to contact the crèche on a regular basis (once a month, for example) to confirm your registration and your motivation. Your child will only be accepted once a place becomes free and your child is able to go to the crèche (after having received all their vaccinations, and so on).

HOW CAN I GET OVER THE BABY BLUES?

Around three to four days after giving birth, while you thought that you would be over the moon with happiness, you feel sad and burst into tears without any apparent reason; you feel irritable, overwhelmed and out of your depth... You are going through the baby blues, a period of time after giving birth which is so frequent that it is considered normal. It is due to a combination of fatigue and a sudden drop in hormones after the birth in an already very emotional time. It generally lasts no more than 15 days.

- Do not isolate yourself, and ask for help without feeling guilty: get your partner, family or friends to give you a hand. They can help you to relax by preparing you a meal or two, going shopping for you or doing some household tasks so you do not have to.
- Do not be afraid to talk about it. Do not worry if you break down and begin to cry. Express your feelings.
- Follow the same rhythm as your baby. Make the most of their naps to have a rest. Know your limits and stick to them.
- Keep tiring visits to a minimum.
- Have faith in yourself: tell yourself that you have the right to hesitate and be unsure of what to do with this little baby that you are still getting to know. We are not born with parenting skills. You will quickly find the best

things to do to take care of your baby.
- Yoga, relaxation and sophrology can all be of some help.

If the baby blues lasts for more than 15 days, see your doctor, because 10 to 20% of new mothers develop postnatal depression, which requires medical and psychological treatment.

HOW SHOULD I PREPARE MYSELF IF I HAVE TWINS?

Not just one, but two babies to handle! Although this may seem overwhelming, the key, as always, is in the organisation.

- Buy double the supplies. There are double buggies and prams for walks. Build up a large stock of nappies, clothes and bottles. Buy two sets of bottles in different colours so you can quickly see how much each baby has drunk.
- It is a good idea to use a notebook or a table to draw yourself a checklist, so you know who has taken what at what time (milk, medication...). This is especially useful when you are tired, because you forget things much more easily. Today, you can also download very useful ap-

plications for your phone, such as Baby Care, Baby Manager and Nestlé Baby.

- Base your own rhythm on that of your children as much as possible, so you can grab some much-needed rest whenever you can.
- Both parents have to be involved in the process, whether caring for the babies or seeing to the house. However, do not forget to take some time for yourselves, because your hectic everyday lives can make you forget about each other and destroy your intimacy.
- If you have identical twins and you are afraid that you will confuse them, put a bit of nail varnish on one of the baby's toes. Do not worry though – you will soon learn to tell them apart.
- If both of you are feeding the babies, make sure you take turns, because they both need maternal contact when they are being fed.
- If you are breastfeeding your children and they are both hungry at the same time, feed the one who seems the most impatient first. However, you could try feeding them both at the same time if you feel up to the challenge: some mothers manage to do just that.
- However, do not try the same thing when

changing and washing them: do one child at a time.
- If both babies begin to cry at the same time, do not panic and do not feel guilty: your children will quickly learn to be patient.

Unfortunately, unlike in some countries like Belgium, the amount of statutory maternity leave in the UK is the same for all pregnant women – 52 weeks. It does not matter how many children you are expecting. However, you may be able to get a Sure Start Maternity Grant if you are expecting a multiple birth, have children already and already receive some benefits.

THEY ARE TWINS, NOT CLONES!

- Avoid similar names (such as Tim and Tom, for example) and identical clothing, because this will make it harder for them to develop their own personality and identity.
- Do not always address them in the same order in order to avoid making one of them feel inferior.
- Do not call them "the twins", because

being constantly associated with their brother or sister can lead to feelings of frustration that they are not appreciated as their own person.

WHAT WILL HAPPEN IF MY BABY IS PREMATURE?

If your baby is born before your 37th week, they are considered to be premature. If they are seriously premature, a paediatrician is asked to be at the birth in order to see to the newborn as soon as they are born. The premature baby will then be transferred to a neonatal unit where they will be put in an incubator and monitored closely. If the newborn is too underdeveloped, they will need to be given a respirator, be fed with a nasogastric tube or a drip, be put under cardiac monitoring and placed under a lamp to prevent the development of jaundice. Of course, you can visit them and hold them as soon as possible. In the meantime, do not be afraid to talk to them, touch them, or give them a toy or a tissue that smells like you. If you want to, bring them some of your milk.

Many premature babies leave the hospital on more or less the same day as the initial due date. If your child is seriously premature, a hospital paediatrician will continue to keep an eye on them to detect any possible psychomotor development problems, sensory difficulties, and so on.

WHAT ARE THE OBLIGATORY VACCINATIONS FOR BABIES?

The principle of vaccinations is to introduce an external agent (an antigen) into the organism in order to stimulate the production of antibodies, allowing them to protect themselves against infection without actually causing the illness. Vaccinations offer collective protection, because the more people are vaccinated, the less chance the microbe will spread. Although vaccinations are not compulsory in the UK, they are strongly recommended: any parents who are unsure about the risks of vaccinations should take some time to make an informed decision.

Most nursery schools in the UK do not require proof of vaccination but, again, parents are advised to protect their children against all the diseases that they can.

Your baby will receive their first vaccination at the age of 8 weeks, after which they should follow the NHS vaccination schedule.

HOW CAN I PREPARE MY OLDER CHILDREN FOR THE ARRIVAL OF THEIR NEW BROTHER OR SISTER?

The best way to tell your older child about the arrival of their little brother or sister is after the fourth month of your pregnancy, when you are alone together, with simple words. Tell them that they were inside mummy's tummy too. If you have ultrasound scans from this time, show them to them, as well as photos from just after they were born. In their little heads, a new brother or sister means someone new to play with; they find it difficult to understand what a baby really is. There are also some good books explaining pregnancy to children which you can look through together.

Tell them that this birth will change their lives, but make sure not to frighten them. Show them that you love them by giving them lots of cuddles, because they will quickly realise that they no longer have your undivided attention like before. Let them take part in decorating the room, choosing the baby clothes, etc. The more they feel involved, the less they will feel jealous. Help them to express all their emotions and accept them, even if it is difficult for you to hear some of their feelings. You cannot change what your child thinks.

Jealousy is natural, and it can begin with the pregnancy or only appear a few weeks after the birth. In this case, it is up to the parents to help their eldest to get over it. There is no point in telling them off and making them feel guilty, because the child is in a state of extreme distress and needs to be reassured and feel loved. Tell them that they do not have to love the newborn baby – they do not even know them yet – but that mummy and daddy still love them just as much and have enough room in their hearts for both children. After you give birth, it is important that they come to see you and their new sibling as soon as possible so they do not have the feeling that they are being excluded. During this period, they will bond with their father and become a "big boy" or a "big girl", which you can confirm by showing them that you trust them (for example, by letting them hold the baby – under your discreet supervision – and letting them help you to take care of them).

<u>SOME EXTRA ADVICE</u>

Spend some time alone with your eldest child alone, without their little brother or sister. Try doing some activities only with them (playing, reading, going to the cinema or the pool, going for a walk or a cycle, cooking…). These little moments are essential, because they allow your child to feel that they are a part of the family, loved, appreciated and not excluded and forgotten about with the arrival of this intruder.

HOW CAN I GET MY DOG READY FOR THE ARRIVAL OF THE BABY?

It is a good idea to prepare your dog for the arrival of your baby so it does not get jealous and aggressive, particularly if this is your first baby and the animal previously had all of your attention.

Before coming back from the maternity ward, have a piece of clothing with your baby's smell brought to your house every day, so that your dog will already be familiar with their scent. When you come home, let your dog come up to and sniff the baby – while watching them very carefully – so they will recognise them. Speak to your dog softly and stroke it, but do not let it lick the baby.

FURTHER READING

BIBLIOGRAPHY

- Geberowicz, B. and Deguen, F. (2007) *On attend un nouveau bébé*. Paris: Éditions Albin Michel.

- Monceau, V. (2013) *Bébé et moi – L'essentiel de ce qu'il faut savoir pour bien l'attendre, l'accueillir, l'accompagner*. CreateSpace Independent Publishing Platform.

- Parmentier, B. (2015) Le matériel de bébé, petit guide pour bien choisir. *Brussels: ONE*. [Online]. [Accessed 26 June 2017]. Available from: <http://www.one.be/uploads/tx_ttproducts/datasheet/Brochure_materiel_de_bebe_ONE.pdf>

- Place, M-H. (2012) *60 activités Montessori pour mon bébé*. Paris: Nathan.

- Planiol, F. and Raoul, E. (1996) *NEUF MOIS pour préparer sa naissance*. Vanves: Hachette.

- Van der Kaa, D. (2017) *Stimulating Your Little One's Mind*. Trans. Neal, R. Brussels: Plurilingua Publishing.

ADDITIONAL SOURCES

- Babycentre. (No date) *I'm pregnant with twins. When should my maternity leave start?* [Online]. [Accessed 26 June 2017]. Available from: <https://www.babycentre.co.uk/x1017915/im-pregnant-with-twins-when-should-my-maternity-leave-start>

- Gov.uk. (No date) *Sure Start Maternity Grant.* [Online]. [Accessed 26 June 2017]. Available from: <https://www.gov.uk/sure-start-maternity-grant>